KIDS SPEAK OUT About

IMMIGRATION

#SUPPORT

MAKE A CHANGE!

Opportunity ⭐ BEGINNINGS

A NEW PLACE!

KIDS CARE! #BELONG #SpeakUp

CHRIS SCHWAB

Rourke
Educational Media

A Division of
Carson
Dellosa
Education

Before Reading: *Building Background Knowledge and Vocabulary*

Building background knowledge can help children process new information and build upon what they already know. Before reading a book, it is important to tap into what children already know about the topic. This will help them develop their vocabulary and increase their reading comprehension.

Questions and Activities to Build Background Knowledge:

1. Look at the front cover of the book and read the title. What do you think this book will be about?
2. What do you already know about this topic?
3. Take a book walk and skim the pages. Look at the table of contents, photographs, captions, and bold words. Did these text features give you any information or predictions about what you will read in this book?

Vocabulary: *Vocabulary Is Key to Reading Comprehension*

Use the following directions to prompt a conversation about each word.

- Read the vocabulary words.
- What comes to mind when you see each word?
- What do you think each word means?

Vocabulary Words:
- ambassador
- citizens
- deported
- flee
- international
- poverty
- refugees
- undocumented

During Reading: *Reading for Meaning and Understanding*

To achieve deep comprehension of a book, children are encouraged to use close reading strategies. During reading, it is important to have children stop and make connections. These connections result in deeper analysis and understanding of a book.

 Close Reading a Text

During reading, have children stop and talk about the following:

- Any confusing parts
- Any unknown words
- Text to text, text to self, text to world connections
- The main idea in each chapter or heading

Encourage children to use context clues to determine the meaning of any unknown words. These strategies will help children learn to analyze the text more thoroughly as they read.

When you are finished reading this book, turn to the next-to-last page for **Text-Dependent Questions** and an **Extension Activity**.

Table of Contents

What Is Immigration?

When people move to a new country, it's called immigration. Immigration is not new. It has been around for a very long time.

Members of your family were probably immigrants at one time. Maybe your great-grandparents came from Russia. Or maybe your family moved from Pakistan just a few years ago. They made the journey to a new country to start over. Families leave home for many reasons, including war, **poverty**, or to find a better life.

These immigrants came to the United States in the early 1900s. The bags they carried were often all they had to start a new life.

Immigration Problems in the United States

Immigrants do not become **citizens** in their new countries right away. Each country has different rules. Because of immigration, some people in the same family might be citizens of different countries.

Take Sophie Cruz's family, for example. Her parents came to the United States from Mexico. They are not U.S. citizens. Sophie and her sister were born in the U.S., so the rules say that they are citizens. Sophie worried every day that her parents would be **deported** back to Mexico because they are not U.S. citizens.

Families May Be Separated

Sophie Cruz is one of more than four million children who live in the U.S. with an **undocumented** parent. Children may be sent to foster homes or left with relatives if their parents are deported.

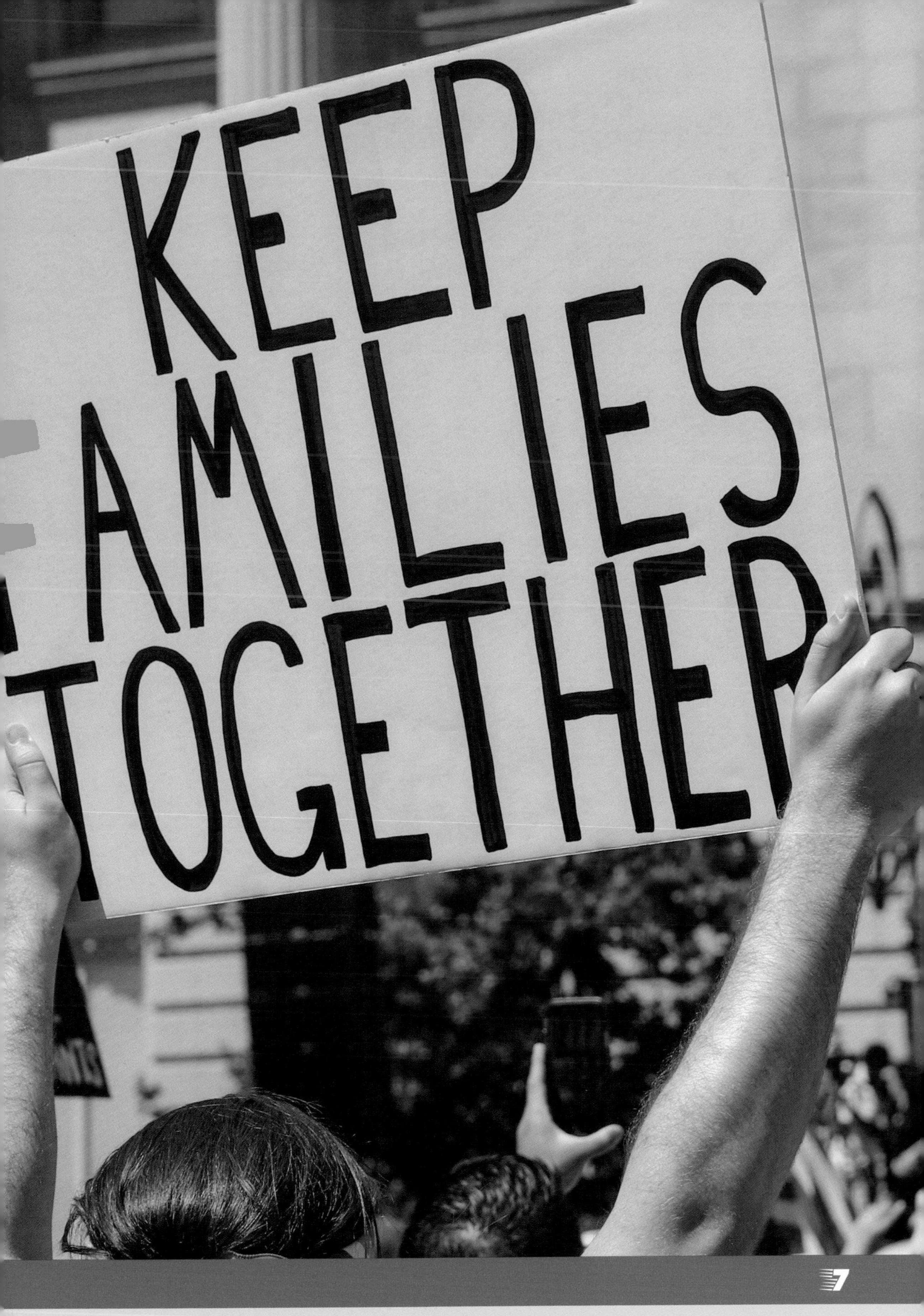
KEEP
AMILIES
TOGETHER

Sophie saw other families separated by deportation. She was afraid every day. Sophie decided to speak out.

When Sophie was five years old, she wrote a letter about immigration to Pope Francis. She saw him in a parade. Guards were all around the important leader. But Sophie got through! The pope stopped the parade. He gave her a hug. She gave him her letter and a T-shirt. The T-shirt had a message asking Pope Francis to help families like hers.

"I believe I have the right to live with my parents," Sophie said after she met with the pope. "All immigrants just like my dad feed this country. They deserve to live with dignity. They deserve to live with respect."

Making a Difference

Sophie didn't stop with Pope Francis. Since then, she has met with President Obama, appeared at the U.S. Supreme Court, and spoke out at the 2017 Women's March.

Some kids immigrated to the United States with their parents. The rules say they are not citizens. Many of them don't remember the countries they were born in. They might think of the U.S. as their home. They're afraid of being deported. They don't want to leave their homes or schools. These kids are often called "Dreamers." Many young Dreamers have found the courage to speak out.

Dreaming of Citizenship

The DREAM Act is an idea for a law. The DREAM Act would give kids who came to the U.S. under the age of 18 a way to become citizens. Though it has a lot of support, it has never become a law.

Immigration Is Hard on Kids

Families in war zones often have to leave their countries quickly. They may escape with nothing but the clothes on their backs. They may not have money or food. They might move in with relatives. They might have to live in a tent. They are **refugees**. It's not easy for a kid to be a refugee. They have left their homes, friends, and schools behind.

Mohamad Al Jounde was forced to **flee** his home country, Syria, during a war. He and his family went to the country of Lebanon to live in a refugee camp. They were safe, but Mohamad was unhappy. He couldn't forget the fear of the war.

Then, Mohamad learned how to take photos. Photography gave Mohamad a way to feel better. It helped him show what he was feeling, and how he lived, without words. He started teaching photography to kids in the refugee camp.

Mohamad Al Jounde gives a speech.

He wanted to give all kids a way to heal. He thought
education was the best way to do it. The refugee camp had
no school. So, 12-year-old Mohamad made a plan to start
one. His family helped. The school soon had more than 200
students. Mohamad taught math and photography!

Let's Hear It for Mohamad!

Mohamad was awarded the **International** Children's Peace Prize
for starting a school in a refugee camp. In his acceptance speech,
he spoke about the strength of refugee children.

At age 14, Muzoon Almellehan also had to flee Syria with her family. With fighting and soldiers everywhere, it was not safe. Muzoon could take only one bag. What do you think she packed? Muzoon took nothing but schoolbooks! Muzoon and her family went to a refugee camp. They lived in a tent with no electricity, water, or internet. But, they were safe.

Muzoon was overjoyed to discover a school in the camp! But many kids did not attend. Muzoon found her mission. Every evening, she went from tent to tent. She told parents and children about the importance of school.

Muzoon became a UNICEF Goodwill **Ambassador**, the youngest one ever. She traveled around refugee camps speaking about the importance of attending school. She has talked to world leaders about providing schools for refugees.

Just like Sophie, Mohamad, and Muzoon, you can speak out! Join these activists and make the world a welcoming place.

"I meet lots of refugees who think that it's a bad thing, a bad name. For me? No. For me, a refugee name gives me strength to create a bright future from my hard situation. We are not weak people. We are strong people. We are not just refugees, we are not just children—we can make a change. I know the change is difficult, but not impossible."

Muzoon Almellehan

1 Contact your representative in Congress. Ask them to support immigrants and refugees.

2 Organize a fundraiser. Donate the money to a charity that helps immigrants.

3 Ask an adult to help you find petitions to sign that support the rights of immigrants.

4 Plan a textbook drive. Ship the books to a refugee camp.

5 Spread awareness about an organization that helps refugees all over the world.

6 Write a pledge titled "I stand with immigrants." See how many signatures you can collect.

7 Ask your teacher to start a pen-pal club with refugee kids. Learn from them.

8 Stay informed! Stay up-to-date on the latest news about immigration.

9 When you see someone being bullied because they are from another country, make it stop.

10 Make an acrostic poem about being welcoming with the word NEIGHBOR.

Glossary

ambassador (am-BAS-uh-dur): the top person sent to represent a group or country

citizens (SIT-i-zuhnz): people who are members of a country

deported (di-PORT-id): sent back to their own country

flee (flee): to run away

international (in-tur-NASH-uh-nuhl): involving more than one country

poverty (PAH-vur-tee): the state of being poor

refugees (ref-yoo-JEEZ): people who are forced to leave home because of war, mistreatment, or a natural disaster

undocumented (un-DOK-yu-men-tid): without legal paperwork toward citizenship

Index

Text-Dependent Questions

1. Name three reasons for immigration.

2. Name three problems immigrants might have.

3. Why is it important to become a citizen in a new country?

4. What are three ways to speak out about immigration rights?

5. What do Sophie, Mohamad, and Muzoon have in common?

Extension Activity

Get a flat map of the world or of your country. Talk to different members of your family, especially older relatives. Find out where they were born—what city, state, province, or country. Mark it on the map. Ask where their parents and grandparents were born. Mark it on the map. Ask questions to figure out where they moved from and to—and why.

About the Author

Chris Schwab is a writer and editor. She has written many articles for newspapers and magazines. Now she writes books for kids. She likes the idea of a world without borders, where people are welcome in any country if they are good citizens. She believes that all people benefit from experiencing other cultures.

Quote sources: Alicia A. Caldwell, "Immigration group planned girl's encounter with Pope Francis for a year," PBS News Hour, WOSU PBS, September 25, 2015: https://www.pbs.org/newshour/nation/immigration-group-planned-girls-encounter-pope-francis-year; "Muzoon Almellehan Goodwill Ambassador," unicef, https://www.unicef.org.uk/celebrity-supporters/muzoon-almellehan/

www.rourkeeducationalmedia.com

PHOTO CREDIT: Cover, p1 ©ronniechua, ©Nikada, ©calvindexter, ©Hulinska_©Yevhenila, ©Bubushonok, ©ulimi; p4 ©komisar; p5 ©Library of Congress; p6 ©FeelPic; p7 ©www.eddie-hernandez.com; p8 ©Rena Schild; p9 ©Matailong Du; p10 ©Joseph Sohm; p11 ©Cory Seamer; p12 ©By bakdc; p13 ©Diego G Diaz; p14 ©cloverphoto; p15 ©thomas koch; p16 ©ahmad zikri, ©Sylvia Lederer; p17 ©Joel Carillet; p18 ©Istvan Csak; p20 ©a katz. ©M.Moira.

Edited by: Hailey Scragg
Cover and interior layout by: Kathy Walsh

Library of Congress PCN Data

Kids Speak Out About Immigration / Chris Schwab
(Kids Speak Out)
ISBN 978-1-73163-856-4 (hard cover)(alk. paper)
ISBN 978-1-73163-933-2 (soft cover)
ISBN 978-1-73164-010-9 (e-Book)
ISBN 978-1-73164-087-1 (ePub)
Library of Congress Control Number: 2020930197

Rourke Educational Media
Printed in the United States of America
01-1942011937